YOU CAN BE WHATEVER YOU WANT TO BE

Career Exploration Writing Primer

By Raven Durant-Smith and Cairo Hunter

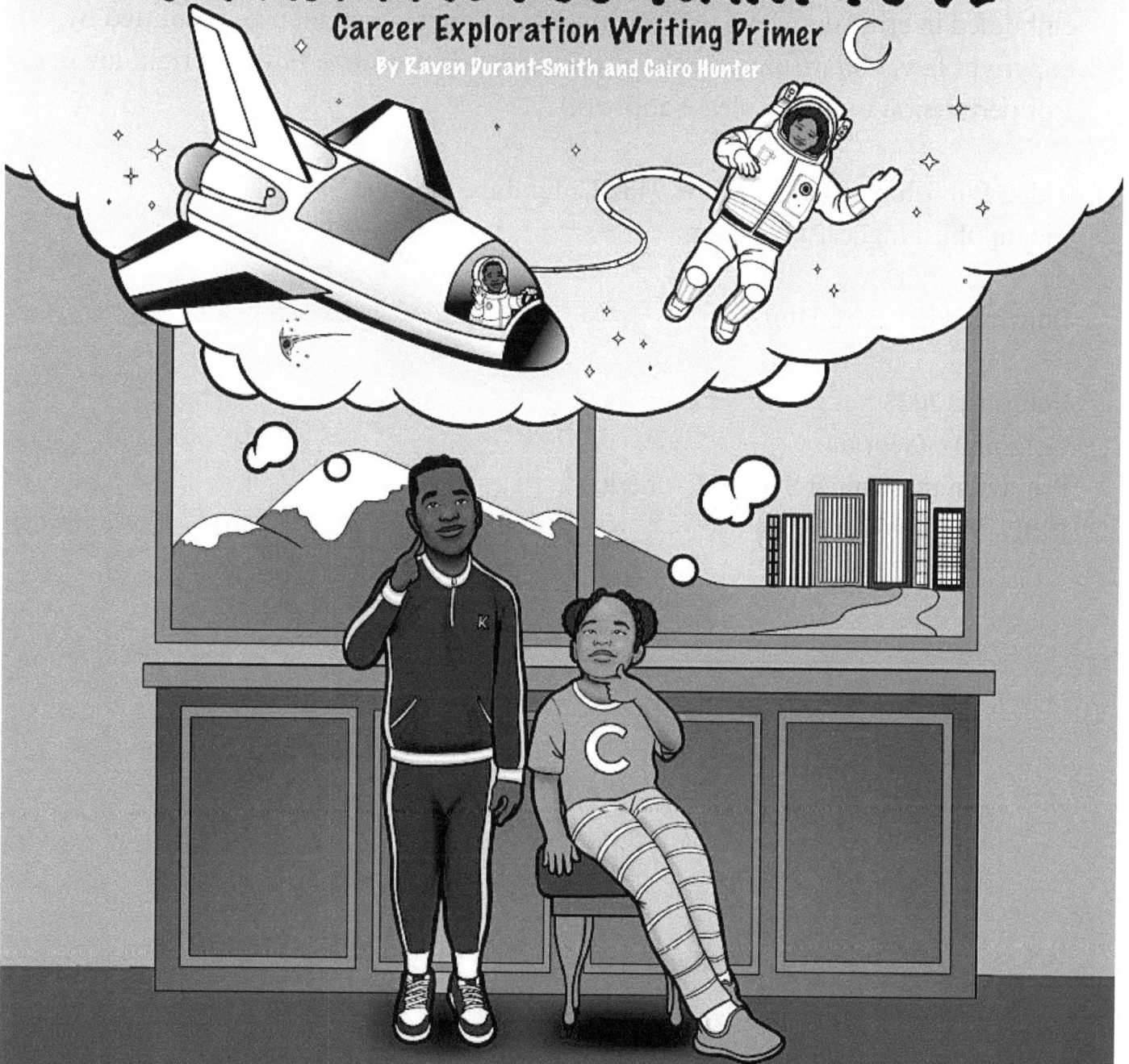

Columbus, GA

Tidan Publishing LLC P.O. Box 9482 Columbus, Georgia 31907
Tidanpublishingllc@gmail.com

Illustrated by Cairo Hunter

Published 2023
Columbus, Georgia
Printed in the United States of America
ISBN: 978-1-960972-08-8

THIS BOOK BELONGS TO

_____

- -

_____

⎯⎯⎯⎯⎯

To Parents/Guardians:

In purchasing this career exploration writing primer you have made a great investment in your child. This book serves to reinforce handwriting skills. Children no longer receive the necessary writing practice in schools; however, this is still a very important and necessary skill. Secondly, children are not aware of the many careers available to them outside of the more traditional ones; therefore, this book introduces attainable career goals that children may not consider early on. Lastly, this book highlights African American career trailblazers to be admired.

DEDICATION

To every child who finds this book in his or her hands, be inspired to be whatever you want to be. And, especially to my God-daughter Cali Durant and step-son Kingston Smith as they start their writing journey.

- Raven

To my five daughters Jordyn, Nuraya, Ayvah, Horizon, and Naomi. Know that the possibilities of life are limitless, challenges are simply moments to learn and grow, and success will be the result of hard work and determination.

- Cairo

Aa

Astronaut

A A A A A A A A A A A A A A A A A A A A A A A A

a a a a a a a a a a a a a a a a a a a a a a a a a a a a

I can be an astronaut like
Mae Jemison!

Bb

Biochemist

BBBBBBBBBBBBBBBBBBBBBBBBBBBBBBB

bbbbbbbbbbbbbbbbbbbbbbbbbb

I can be a biochemist like
Marie Maynard Daly!

Cc

Congressman

C C C C C C C C C C C C C C C C C C C C C C C C C

C C C C C C C C C C C C C C C C C C C C C C C C C C

I can be a Congressman like John Lewis!

Dd

Doctor

D D D D D D D D D D D D D D D D D D D D D

d d d d d d d d d d d d d d d d d d d d d d d d

I can be a doctor like

Charles Drew!

Ee

Environmentalist

EEEEEEEEEEEEEEEEEEEEEEEEEEEEEEEEEEEEEEEE

eeeeeeeeeeeeeeeeeeeeeeeeeeeeeeeeeeeeeeee

I can be an environmentalist
like MaVynee Betsch!

Ff

Fashion Designer

FFFFFFFFFFFFFFFFFFFFFFFFFFFFFFFFFFFF

ffffffffffffffffffffffffffffffffffffffffffffff

I can be a fashion designer

like Ann Lowel

Gg   Gaming Designer

G G G G G G G G G G G G G G G G G G G G G G G G

g g g g g g g g g g g g g g g g g g g g g g g g g g

I can be a gaming designer
like Gerald Lawson!

Hh Hair Care Professional

H H H H H H H H H H H H H H H H H H H H H H H H H H H H H H

h h h h h h h h h h h h h h h h h h h h h h h h h h h h h

I can be a hair care professional
like Madam C.J. Walker!

Ii

I I I I I I I I I I I I I I I I I I I I I I I I I

i i i i i i i i i i i i i i i i i i i i i i i i i i i i i i i

I can be an illustrator like

Jerry Pickney!

Jj

Journalist

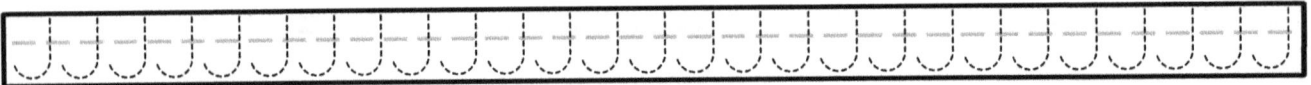

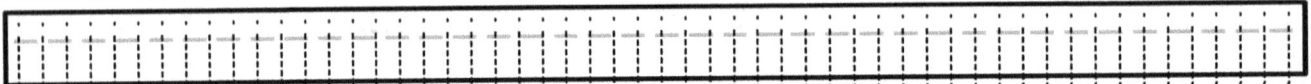

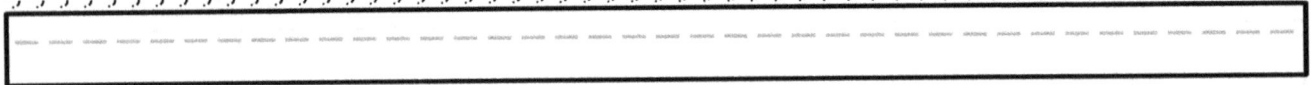

I can be a journalist like
Simeon Booker!

Kk

Kicker

K K K K K K K K K K K K K K K K K K K K K K

k k k k k k k k k k k k k k k k k k k k k k k k k k

I can be a kicker like
Marquette King!

Ll

Lawyer

L L L L L L L L L L L L L L L L L L L L L L L L L L

l l l l l l l l l l l l l l l l l l l l l l l l l l l l l l l l l

I can be a lawyer like
Ben Crump!

Mm

Meteorologist

M M M M M M M M M M M M M M M M M M M M M M

m m m m m m m m m m m m m m m m m m m m

I can be a meteorologist
like Charles E. Anderson!

Nn

Newscaster

NNNNNNNNNNNNNNNNNNNNNNNNNNNNNNNN

nnnnnnnnnnnnnnnnnnnnnnnnnnnnnn

I can be a newscaster
like Fred Blankenship!

Oo

Orthodontist

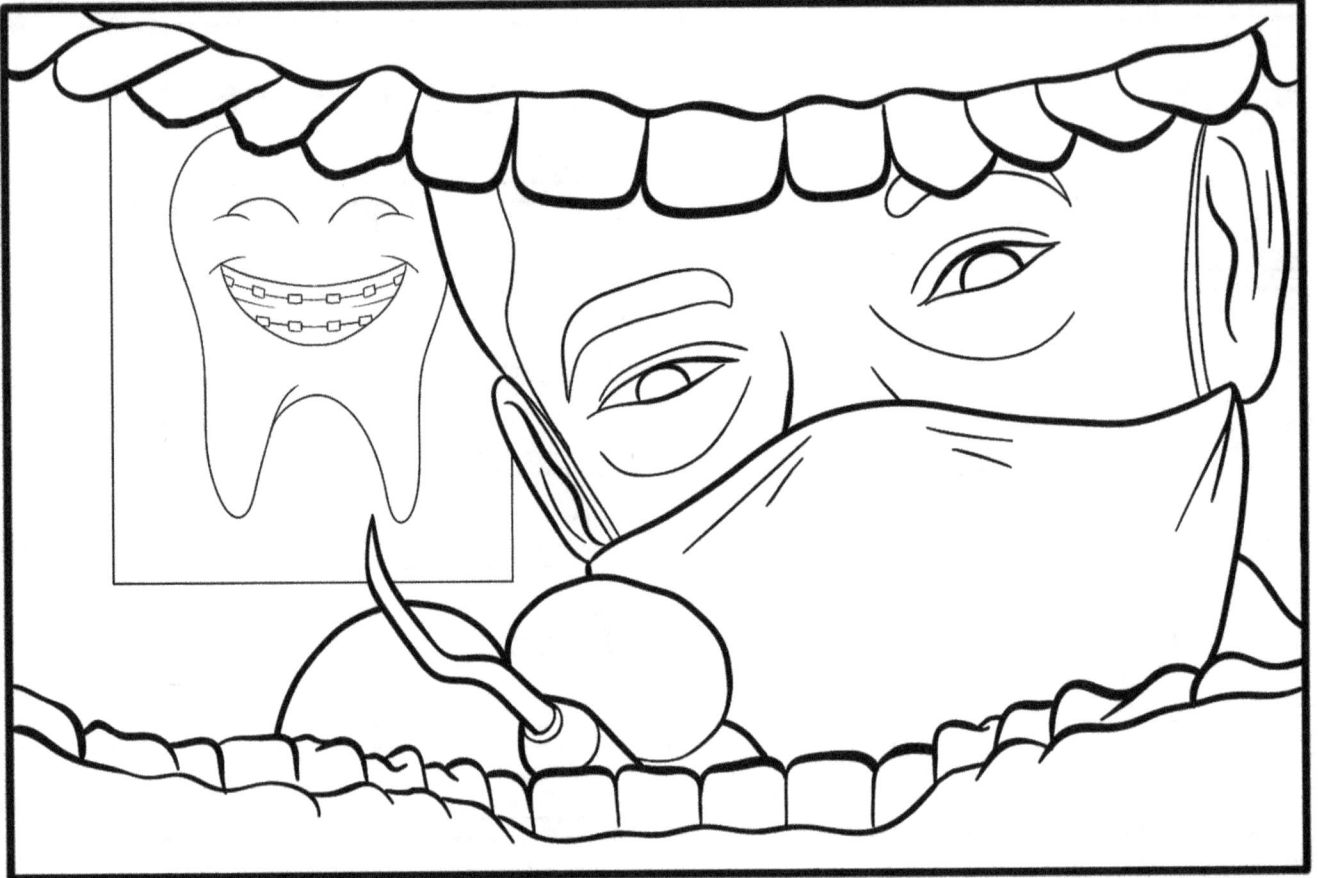

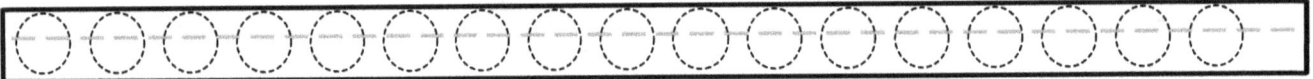

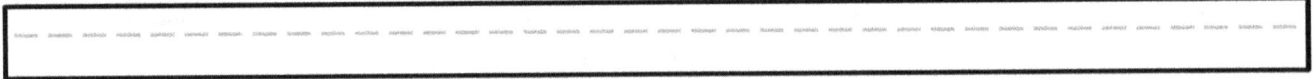

O O O O O O O O O O O O O O O O O O O O O O

O O O O O O O O O O O O O O O O O O O O O O O O

I can be an orthodontist
like Wendell Cotton!

P p

Pianist

P P P P P P P P P P P P P P P P P P P P P P P P P P

p p p p p p p p p p p p p p p p p p p p p p p p p

I can be a pianist like

Kris Bowers!

Qq

Quilter

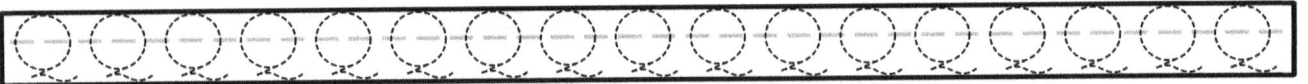

I can be a quilter like
Harriet Powers!

Rr   Radio Personality

R R R R R R R R R R R R R R R R R R R R R R R R R

r r r r r r r r r r r r r r r r r r r r r r r r r r r r

I can be a radio personality
like Tom Joyner!

Ss   Supreme Court Justice

SSSSSSSSSSSSSSSSSSSSSSSSS

sssssssssssssssssssssssss

I can be a Supreme Court
Justice like Ketanji Brown
Jackson!

Tt

Teacher

T T T T T T T T T T T T T T T T T T T T T T T T T T T T T T

t t t t t t t t t t t t t t t t t t t t t t t t t t t t t t t t t t

I can be a teacher like
Fanny Jackson Coppin!

Uu

U U U U U U U U U U U U U U U U U U U U U U

u u u u u u u u u u u u u u u u u u u u u u u u u u

I can be an umpire like
Emmett Ashford!

Vv

Vice President

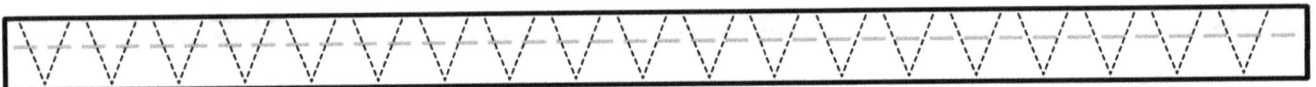

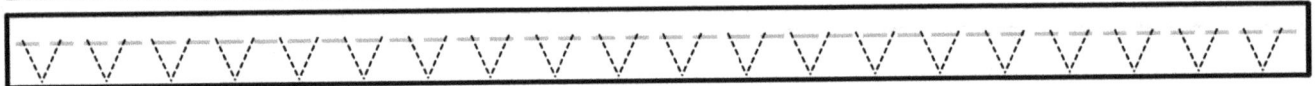

VVVVVVVVVVVVVVVVVVVVVVVVVVVVVVVVVVVVVV

v v v v v v v v v v v v v v v v v v v v v v v v v v

I can be a Vice President
like Kamala Harris!

Ww

Writer

W W W W W W W W W W W W

w w w w w w w w w w w w w w

I can be a writer like

Maya Angelou!

Xx

X-Ray Technician

XXXXXXXXXXXXXXXXXXXXXXXXXX

X X X X X X X X X X X X X X X X X X X X

I can be a x-ray technician
like William Edward Allen, Jr.!

Yy

Yoga Instructor

Y Y Y Y Y Y Y Y Y Y Y Y Y Y Y Y Y Y Y Y Y Y Y Y Y Y Y

u u u u u u u u u u u u u u u u u u u u u u u u u u u u u u u u

I can be a yoga instructor
like Jana Long!

Zz

Zoologist

Z Z Z Z Z Z Z Z Z Z Z Z Z Z Z Z Z Z Z Z Z Z

z z z z z z z z z z z z z z z z z z z z z z z z z z z

I can be a zoologist like
Roger Arliner Young!

Tidan Publishing
l.l.c

www.tidanpublishingllc.com